Read and Play
Ships

by Jim Pipe

Stargazer Books

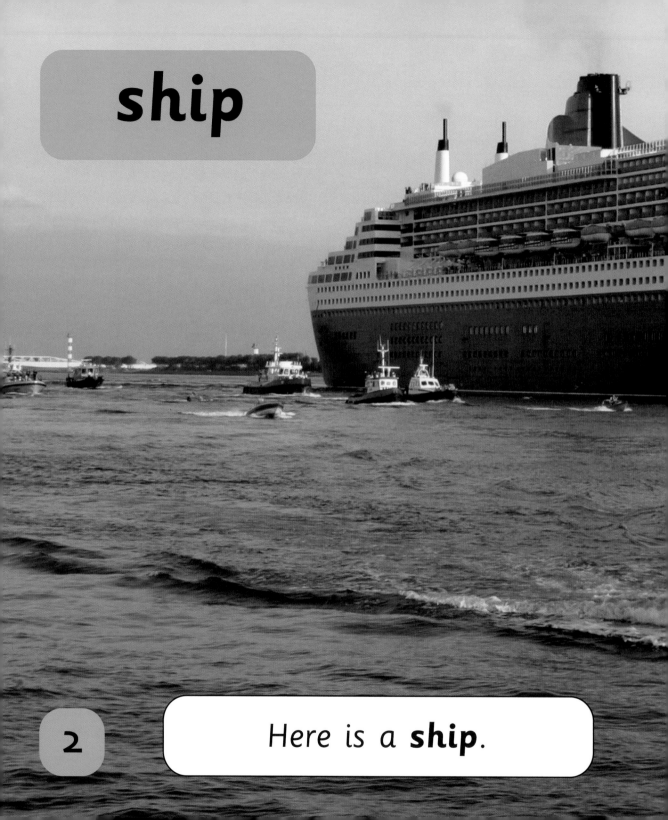

ship

2

Here is a **ship**.

A **ship** is a big boat.

3

hull

4

A ship has a **hull**.

This ship has two **hulls**.

5

deck

This ship has a big **deck**.

6

Planes land
on the **deck**.

7

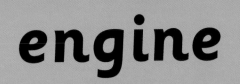

engine

A ship has big **engines**.

propeller

Engines turn a **propeller**.

sails

This ship has **sails**.

Sails make a ship move.

sailor

Sailors sail a ship.

anchor

A ship drops its **anchor** to stop.

13

port

14

A ship stops in a **port**.

Ships are safe in a **port**.

15

fishing

A **fishing** boat is small.

tanker

A **tanker** is enormous.

submarine

This is a **submarine**.

It can go
underwater.

What am I?

anchor

hull

propeller

sails

20

Match the words and pictures.

How many?

Can you count the red ships?

21

What job?

Tanker

Cargo ship

Ferry

Fishing boat

22

What jobs do these ships do?

Index

Can you find these
pictures of ships
in this book?

For Parents and Teachers

Questions you could ask:

p. 2 Where would you see a ship? e.g. at sea, in a port, on a big river. Ask what boats/ships the reader has seen, e.g. ferry, yacht, canoe, pirate ship.

p. 4 What are ships made from? Ships today are made of metal. In the past ships were made of wood.

p. 6 What is this ship called? It is called an aircraft carrier because it carries aircraft. It has a very big deck so that planes can land on it. Most ships have a deck, the flat part on top of a ship that you can walk on, e.g. the deck on a ferry.

p. 9 What makes a big ship move? The engines make the propeller spin. This pushes a ship forward. To go backward, the propellers spin the other way.

p.10 How many sails can you see? Explain how sails work: when the wind blows against a sail, it pushes a boat forward. Ask the reader to blow a feather or a ping pong ball across a bowl of water.

p. 13 What is an anchor for? A heavy anchor sinks to the bottom and stops a ship from floating away.

p. 14 What can you see in a port? e.g. tall cranes to unload cargo, tug helping a big ship to dock.

p.18 If you were in a submarine underwater, what could you see? Ask reader to describe what is under the water, e.g. sea animals, seabed.

Activities you could do:

• Ask readers to describe or imagine a journey in a boat, e.g. wind and waves, rocking of the boat, sounds, getting splashed! You could use this as an opportunity to discuss water safety.

• Encourage puddle or water play, e.g. watching ripples/waves, seeing what objects float or sink, and testing how deep water is using a stick.

• Role play: Get readers to sit in a circle and "row" a boat while singing "Row, row, row your boat."

• Help the reader to cut out or collect pictures of different boats, e.g. fishing boats, pirate ships.

• Make boats/rafts from plastic plates, egg boxes, paper. Explore which materials work best.

© Aladdin Books Ltd 2008

Designed and produced by
Aladdin Books Ltd

All rights reserved

Printed in the United States

Series consultant
Zoe Stillwell is an experienced preschool teacher.

First published in 2008
in the United States
by Stargazer Books
c/o The Creative Company
123 South Broad Street
P.O. Box 227
Mankato, Minnesota 56002

Photocredits:
*l-left, r-right, b-bottom, t-top,
c-center, m-middle*
All photos from istockphoto.com except: 5, 23 mtl—Richard Bennett, Courtesy Incat. 12, 13, 6-7, 18-19, 20br, 23br—US Navy.
21—Courtesy Superfast Ferries.

Library of Congress Cataloging-in-Publication Data

Pipe, Jim, 1966-
   Ships / by Jim Pipe.
      p. cm. -- (Read and play)
   Includes bibliographical references and Index.
   ISBN 978-1-59604-166-0 (alk. paper)
   1. Ships--Juvenile literature. I. Title.

VM150.P56 2007
387.2--dc22

                    2007007760